LITTLE PEOPLE WHO
BECAME GREAT

STATUE OF ABRAHAM LINCOLN—ST. GAUDENS

LITTLE PEOPLE WHO BECAME GREAT

STORIES OF THE LIVES OF THOSE WHOM EVERY CHILD SHOULD KNOW

BY

LAURA ANTOINETTE LARGE

Author of "Old Stories for Young Readers."

NEW YORK

THE PLATT & MUNK CO., INC.

NOTE

Author and publisher wish to express their appreciation to Underwood and Underwood, the *Youth's Companion*, and Gramstorff Bros. Inc., for the use of copyrighted pictures used in illustrating this volume.

CONTENTS

Little People Who Became Great

A BOY WHO SPENT THREE YEARS IN
A PALACE

WHEN Michael Angelo was a little boy he thought more about drawing than of any other thing in all the world. His father sent him to school but Michael Angelo did not like books and would not study hard. He drew pictures on his books, instead. "I want to learn to draw," he would say to his father.

His father was angry at this. "I do not want you to be an artist, my son," he said. "Artists cannot earn much money and I do not want you to become one."

Poor little Michael Angelo did not want much money. He only wanted to learn to draw well, and he could not get the idea out of his head.

"I would rather do this than any other thing," he told his father.

Michael Angelo's best friend knew a great artist. Often the great artist would let the two boys watch him draw. This made Michael Angelo more eager than ever.

One day the artist went to Michael Angelo's father. "I will pay you for the boy's work if you will let him study with me," he said.

The father was willing to do this, and Michael Angelo studied with the artist for three years.

At that time there lived a prince who loved beautiful statues. He liked them so well he sent all over the world to get the very best there were. This prince was a kind man. He thought it would be well if others could enjoy his fine statues.

He said to the drawing teachers of the city in which he lived, "Choose your two best pupils. Send them to study my fine statues. I will get a teacher to help them."

All the drawing pupils in the city of Florence

wanted to see the prince's statues. But only two could be chosen from each class.

One teacher had two bright pupils. They were great friends and both could draw well. It was not hard for this teacher to make his choice. Michael Angelo and his friend were the lucky ones.

You may be sure there were some happy boys in Florence, that day. And Michael Angelo was the happiest of them all. He was always glad to see beautiful things and to learn about them.

While visiting the kind prince, Michael Angelo first spent his time in drawing. Then one day he saw a young man modeling in clay. Michael Angelo thought that he would like this work even better than drawing, and it was not long before he was working in clay, also.

One day, Michael Angelo was making a faun's head. The prince came along and saw him at work. "That is a fine head," the prince said. "But you have made one mistake. The faun should have one tooth missing."

Michael Angelo did not say much. When the

prince came around a second time the faun had one tooth less than it had had before. Michael Angelo had changed the head to make it just as it should be.

The prince was much pleased. "My boy," he said. "I see that you are willing to learn. You may come and live with me in my palace. I will get you a teacher and you shall study with my three sons."

Again Michael Angelo was a happy boy, and for three years he worked in the palace, with princes for friends. He spent most of his time carving in marble, now, and his work was becoming more and more beautiful. Indeed, many people said, "Some day Michael Angelo will be a great sculptor."

After Michael Angelo had lived at the palace for three years, the kind prince died. Michael Angelo had lost a friend but he had not lost his love for the work. He kept on and on, until he became one of the greatest sculptors that has ever lived.

The people of Florence, Italy, had a huge block

of marble. One man had tried to carve a giant out of it, but had failed. The people asked Michael Angelo to do something with it.

"I will see what I can do," Michael Angelo promised them. Then he carved and carved, for eighteen months. When he had finished, you could see that a wonderful sculptor had done the work. The huge block was changed into a young man with a sling-shot thrown over his shoulder. He was going forth to fight a giant. It was David, the shepherd boy. Forty men worked four days to move it, and it is a wonder that it did not take longer. It weighed eighteen thousand pounds, or just nine tons!

Someone said, "What a beautiful piece of sculpture it is! Let us put it at the gate of our city. It will help to keep watch over our people."

This is what the people of Florence did, and for many years David the shepherd boy looked quietly upon all who entered the gates of the city.

At another time Michael Angelo carved the statue of Moses. This statue is in Rome. It looks so real it almost seems to speak, as you stand before it.

Michael Angelo carved many, many more beautiful statues also. Among the statues he carved is one called DAY AND NIGHT, and another is called TWILIGHT AND DAWNING.

Michael Angelo did not spend all of his time as a sculptor. Once in a while he stopped to paint a few beautiful pictures.

In Rome, there is a large church named St. Peter. This church has many parts, one of which is called The Sistine Chapel. The ceiling of this chapel is covered with many pictures. Each picture tells some story about the Bible.

If you have ever watched anyone paint the ceiling in your home, you know how hard it is. Painting walls is a much easier task. Only a very great artist could make the pictures look so real and so beautiful.

If you are ever in Rome or Florence, try to see the wonderful work of Michael Angelo.

THE BOY WHO BUILT CASTLES IN THE AIR

PERHAPS you know what it means to build castles in the air. You keep thinking of great things that you would like to do, or of the fine things that you would like to have.

Some people build castles in the air, but they do not try hard enough to make the play castles turn into real ones. Andrew Carnegie was not that kind of a boy, as you will see.

Andrew Carnegie's father was a weaver until the time when Andrew became ten years of age. Mr. Carnegie and his family lived in a little Scotland town where they were contented and happy.

Then people began to make cloth by machinery and Mr. Carnegie was soon without work. He was very sad when he came home one night. "Andy," he said to his little son. "I will have no more weaving to do. People do not care to give orders for hand-made cloth any more."

It was then that Andrew began to build his castles in the air. How he wished that he might earn some money to give to his father and mother! Even a dollar or two each week would have made Andrew the happiest boy in all of Scotland.

While Andrew was wondering what a little boy of ten years could do to make money, Mr. Carnegie was wondering what he should do to earn a living. He talked it over with his good wife who said that she thought it might be well for the family to go to America to live. Some of their relatives had done this and had been earning a good living in the new country. "Perhaps we can do well, there, too," Mrs. Carnegie said to her husband.

After looking into the matter carefully Mr. Carnegie made up his mind to move to America. A few weeks later the family had settled in Allegheny, Pennsylvania.

Here Mr. Carnegie found work, and Andrew was given a position, also. He became a bobbin-boy in a factory, for which he received $1.25 a week.

Andrew worked hard for this money, but he did not mind hard work. He gave the $1.25 to his mother each week, and his good mother was very glad to get it. At that time Andrew thought that $1.25 was a great deal of money, but he still kept on building his castles in the air. "Some day I will make more money," he said to himself. And this is just what happened.

Before long Andrew was given the position of engine-boy in a factory. It was his duty to fire the engine, and for this he received $1.80 a week. This work was harder than the work that the bobbin-boy had to do, but $1.80 is better than $1.25, as you know. For this reason Andrew gave up his first position and started to work at the second.

It was dark in the engine room where he had to work. There was no daylight and no bright sunshine at all. Andrew went to work early in the morning and did not get home until almost dark. At times Andrew wished that he might see a little more of the sunshine, but he did not say anything about this to his mother. "Some day I will do better," he said to himself.

When Andrew Carnegie was fourteen years old, he was given a chance to do better, just as he had thought. A messenger boy was needed in one of the telegraph offices of the city, and Andrew was offered the position at $2.50 a week.

When Andrew went to the telegraph office and saw how the sun shone into the windows from all sides, he was greatly pleased. The bright sunshiny office was so much better than the dark engine room in which he had been working.

Andrew went to work at the new position, and it was a bright happy looking lad who helped to deliver telegraph messages throughout the city, that year.

Andrew soon learned the names of the business firms along most of the streets of the city so that he might be able to deliver their messages

18

more quickly. Besides this, he learned to operate a telegraph machine.

The Superintendent was pleased when he saw how Andrew went about his work. One day he asked Andrew if he would not like to become a telegraph operator at a salary of $6.25 a week.

Of course you know what Andrew said to this. And perhaps you can imagine how rich he felt when he received his new salary.

You would think that by this time Andrew would have stopped building air castles but he had not. It was a great pleasure to be able to give his mother the $6.25 every week, but he thought that it would be very fine if he could give her more than this.

Andrew worked harder than ever and after many months the Superintendent asked him to help in his private office at a salary of $8.75 a week.

Again you can guess what was Andrew Carnegie's answer. And no doubt you can also guess who became the new Superintendent when the old one was called upon to leave the city after many more months.

At last there came a time when Andrew Carnegie's mother had as much money as she needed and Andrew had a chance to save a part of his earnings.

It would take a long time for you to read all that Andrew did from that time until he became an old man but you will surely want to know what became of all the air castles.

Andrew Carnegie did not remain a Superintendent all of his life. After a few years he became a steel manufacturer and this brought him a great deal of money. He earned so much that his mother could have a million dollars almost any time she wanted it. His father, too, could have had many fine things if he had only lived long enough to receive them.

Andrew Carnegie's castles were no longer built of air. They were now real ones for all of his wishes had come true.

Andrew Carnegie was a very happy man as

you may suppose. But he did not forget the people who were less fortunate than he. Besides giving to his own family he gave away millions of dollars to strange people. Before the year 1915 had closed Andrew Carnegie had given over $180,000,000 for Public Libraries and other useful things!

THE GIRL WHO BUILT CASTLES IN THE AIR

WHAT would you think if you had a baby sister who could sing the tune of MY COUNTRY 'TIS OF THEE or THE STAR SPANGLED BANNER before she was two years old? Perhaps you would think that she was the smartest sister in the whole country, and this is what she might be.

When little Jenny Lind was only twenty months old she could sing tunes that were just as hard as MY COUNTRY 'TIS OF THEE or THE STAR SPANGLED BANNER. She lived in Sweden and the songs that she sang were the Swedish native airs. Baby Jenny thought that they were very pretty songs. She liked the tunes even though she was too young to say the words that went with them.

After awhile little Jenny grew old enough to sing the words as well as the tunes. Then she would sing and sing. You would have liked to hear little Jenny's songs. Her voice was as clear and as sweet as the voice of any child you have ever heard.

When Jenny was three years old she was very happy because some soldiers marched by the house every day. Some children would have looked at the soldiers because they liked to see their suits or watch them go LEFT, RIGHT, LEFT, RIGHT. It was not so with little Jenny Lind. She like the soldiers because some of them blew such pretty tunes on their bugles. One tune they blew more than any other and it was not long before little Jenny had learned to sing it.

One day when she thought that she was all alone in the house she crept up to the big piano and played one of the soldier's tunes. She had never played the piano before but she had watched her half-sister do so. She found it very easy to pick out the tune with one finger, singing as she played.

Little Jenny thought that she was alone in the

house. She did not know that her grandmother was at home until she heard a voice that called out the name of Jenny's half-sister. Then little Jenny was frightened because she thought that her grandmother might be angry. Little Jenny was so young that she had never been allowed to play on the piano and she did not know what her grandmother would think of it. So she hid underneath the big piano and kept very, very still. If little Jenny had been older she would have known that it does not take very sharp eyes to find someone hidden under a piano. The grandmother came into the room and saw little Jenny at once. She said to her, "Child, was that you singing and playing the pretty tune?" Little Jenny had tears in her eyes as she answered that she was the one. She was surprised to see that her grandmother was pleased and not angry.

The grandmother took Jenny from her hiding place, and when the mother came home the grandmother told her that some day she would have a great singer for a daughter. "Mark my words," she said. "Some day this child will bring you help." By this she meant that Jenny might be a great singer and earn a good deal of money.

When Jenny was six years old her father and mother became very poor. Jenny's mother had to spend so much of her time earning money that little Jenny was sent away to the home of a man and his wife who had no children and wanted some little girl to live with them.

Jenny's new home was on a busy street and many people passed by the house each day. But there were no children in the house and little Jenny would have been very lonesome if it had not been for one thing. Jenny liked to sing so well that she could not be lonesome. No matter how dark the day might be, there was always a sunny spot around where little Jenny was.

When she was nine years old someone gave her a beautiful cat with a blue ribbon around its neck. Little Jenny thought that her cat was the finest cat in all the world. She would often sit in the window looking out upon the busy street. In her arms she would hold the pet cat while she sang her sweetest songs to him. The cat seemed to like the singing for he would purr and purr. Sometimes he would curl up into a ball and have a good nap.

One day the maid who worked for a Swedish actress passed by the window where little Jenny sat singing to her cat. The maid heard the singing and looked up. She had never heard such a beautiful song on a busy street and it brought tears to her eyes. When the maid found that the song had come from a little nine-year-old girl singing to her cat she hurried home to tell her mistress about it.

The actress found out where little Jenny's mother lived. She asked the mother to bring little Jenny to her. When the actress had heard Jenny sing she was delighted. "A girl with such a voice should be taught to sing on the stage where many people can hear her," she said to Jenny's mother. Then she asked Jenny's mother if she would allow the little girl to study for the stage if someone would give her lessons without charging for the work. The mother did not like to do this at first, but at last she gave her consent and the actress told her to bring Jenny back the next day.

It was then that little Jenny Lind began to build her air castles. How she wished that some-one would be good enough to be her teacher! Little Jenny wanted to learn to sing so well that everyone in the town who heard her would be made happier.

The actress took Jenny to an old music teacher where she sang one of her prettiest songs. The old music teacher was much pleased and would have liked to have taken the little girl for a pupil but he thought that it would be better for her to study with the manager of a theatre. In those days some of the theatres had training schools where children learned how to act, play the piano, or sing pretty songs for the stage. The manager of the theatre had charge of the train-

27

ing school and this was why the old music teacher wanted Jenny to go to him.

Jenny was very much frightened when she found herself before the manager of the theatre. She hoped that he would like her so that he would let her study at his school without paying for it.

The manager was surprised when he saw Jenny. She was a pale, shy looking little girl. He did not think that she could sing well. "You ask a foolish thing," he said to the music master. "Surely this child cannot sing!"

Little Jenny spoke up at once. "May I sing for you?" she asked the manager. The manager said that she might do so and Jenny sang for him the pretty song that she had also sung for the old music master. When the manager had heard the song he was sorry that he had spoken so rudely. "I will take the child," he said. "She may come into my training school and I will teach her how to sing for the stage."

Little Jenny went to the school a few days

later. She had not been there long before she began to feel that she was learning how to sing well enough to make many people of her city happy. Whenever she sang in the school concerts the people always clapped and clapped because her voice was so sweet and so beautiful. This pleased little Jenny but she was not satisfied. She kept on building air castles, wishing that some day she might sing well enough to please the people of even larger cities.

Just as Jenny Lind was wishing this, a sad thing happened. It seems hard to believe, but it is true. Jenny Lind's beautiful voice disappeared one day. No one knew just how it happened. No one knew just how long it would stay away, but her beautiful voice was surely gone! Some people said that she had sung too much for a little girl and that this was why her voice had lost its strength.

Poor Jenny! How sad she was! She could not take singing lessons any more. The teachers told her that she must give her voice a rest if she wished it to come back again.

Then little Jenny went to work to learn to play the piano. She was not sad long because of a voice within her that seemed to say that in time things would come out all right and she would be able to sing again.

For four years Jenny Lind staid at the school taking piano lessons. Then something happened to make Jenny Lind believe that the voice within her had told the truth. She was asked to sing a short solo in a play because no one else wanted to sing it. The manager did not think that Jenny would be able to sing it well, and Jenny Lind, herself, did not think so. But when she tried the song, Oh! Oh! How happy she was! She found that her voice had come back again! It had returned as quickly as it had once disappeared. After waiting four years Jenny Lind found that she could at last sing again!

Jenny's old teacher began at once to give her lessons and she went to work as hard as ever.

After awhile she began to feel that it might be well for her to study in another city, and her teacher told her that she should go to the big city of Paris. Jenny was very glad to do this. She worked for many months giving concerts so that she might earn enough money to study in Paris where many of the best teachers in the world lived.

Again Jenny Lind built air castles. This time she wished that her voice might grow to be so sweet that everyone who heard her in the big city of Paris would be pleased.

Jenny Lind went to study in Paris but her wishes did not come true at once. Another sad thing happened. Once more she lost her voice and had to stop singing for six months, to rest it.

Many people would have surely given up, but it was not so with Jenny Lind. She rested her voice and then went to work again.

And from this time on Jenny Lind had many happy days. Her voice never disappeared again but grew sweeter and stronger and better every day. It grew to be so beautiful that when she sang you would think that a bird was in the room. She could sing as high as any girl in your school and seven or eight notes higher. If there is a piano in your school ask your teacher to play notes above high G and then you will know just how far Jenny Lind could go with her beautiful voice that sounded like that of a bird.

Not only the people of Paris but also the people of Berlin and London, and even the people of America were made very happy when Jenny Lind sang for them. Everyone thought that she was the most beautiful singer in the whole world.

With all this, Jenny Lind was not satisfied until she had taken a great deal of the money that she had earned and given it away to people who needed it. After she had been singing for awhile she began the new plan of giving away a part of the money that she earned, in every place she visited.

When she visited London, she left a large sum of money for one of its hospitals. In America she gave concerts for poor people and would not take any money for them. At one time she helped many of the poor people of Sweden.

Jenny Lind worked hard to make her own wishes come true. But she did not forget the wishes of others.

A BOY LIKE OTHER BOYS IN MANY WAYS

IT is easy to guess what Henry did that most boys like to do. He played ball and flew a kite. Sometimes he went swimming or hunting with his big brother. When the circus came to town, Henry was there. After it was over, there was a good deal of circus at home. His sisters looked on and clapped their hands. They saw such wonderful sights!

Once the circus-rider got hurt. He was riding the wooden horse on the back porch. His sisters must have shouted "Three cheers for the rider! Keep it up! Ride fast!" at any rate, the young rider was making his horse go! Back and forth went the wooden rocking-horse.

Then there was a CRASH! and over went the circus-rider and horse.

The girls cried, "Oh! Oh! Is anyone hurt?"

"Only a neck broken," replied Henry. Of

course the horse was the unlucky one with the broken neck.

In winter there was coasting, skating and riding on sleds. Perhaps someone got hit with a snowball when this boy was around.

On week days there was school. At night he and his sisters sat around the sitting-room table to study. It was so quiet that you could hear the clock tick. When they were through, Hooray! There was a good time until bed-time.

On Sunday Henry went to church, twice. Everyone in the family went unless there was sickness. In those days the churches were not heated well. Henry carried a foot-stove heated with live coals. This was passed along so that everyone could have a turn.

On Sunday afternoons there were Bible stories at home. Henry liked these very well. When there were pictures to go with them, he liked them very, very well.

When Henry was thirteen years old, one thing happened to show that he was not like other boys in every way. Henry heard about a fight between a man and an Indian. It was on the shores of a body of water. Henry wrote a poem about it and called the poem THE BATTLE OF LOVELL'S POND.

Henry did not want any one to know that he had written the poem. He would not tell any one but his sister. "I will tell you if you will promise not to tell," he told his sister.

Henry mailed the poem to a newspaper of the city in which he lived. When the paper came out, Henry and his sister looked for the poem. How happy they were to find that it had been printed!

After this Henry wrote more poems. He worked so hard that in a few years he became a great poet.

Now I will tell you what this poet wrote and then you will know his last name. He wrote HIAWATHA and THE CHILDREN'S HOUR.

Now you surely know what his name is. Yes, it is LONGFELLOW.

WHO BECAME GREAT

Once someone wrote a funny poem for a joke. They said that it was Henry W. Longfellow's first poem. Henry W. Longfellow did not write funny poems and he did not write this one. You may like to read it, just for fun. This is it:—

Mr. Finney had a turnip and it grew behind the barn.
It grew and it grew, and the turnip did no harm.
It grew and it grew until it could grow no taller,
When Mr. Finney took it and put into the cellar.
There it lay, there it lay, until it began to rot,
When his daughter Susie washed it and put it into
    the pot.
Then she boiled it and she boiled it, as long as she
        was able,
When his daughter Lizzie took and put it on the table.
Mr. Finney and his wife both sat down to sup;
They ate and they ate, until they ate the turnip up.

Henry W. Longfellow's poems are better than this one. After you have read about Mr. Finney and his turnip, a few times you are tired of it. Mr. Longfellow's poems are so beautiful, you will like them better the more you read them.

LITTLE PEOPLE

Ask your teacher to read THE CHILDREN'S HOUR or HIAWATHA.

Some children like to learn this part of Hiawatha :—

"Then the little Hiawatha learned of every bird its
   language,
Learned their names and all their secrets;
Where they built their nests in summer,
Where they hid themselves in winter;
Talked with them, whene'er he met them;
Called them 'Hiawatha's Chickens.' "

A BOY WHO WAS NOT LIKE OTHER BOYS IN MANY WAYS

WHEN Thomas Edison was a very little fellow he was missing one morning. His mother could not find him although she had looked almost everywhere about the house and garden. At last she thought of the barn and went to look for Thomas there.

What do you thing she saw when she reached the barn? She saw her son sitting on a nest of goose eggs because he thought that he could hatch them out more quickly than the goose mother.

Now you know what happened to the eggs. Almost every shell broke and not one egg turned into a little goose. Thomas was sorry to think that Mrs. Goose could do so much better than he, but he was glad that he had learned something new about hatching.

That was the way it was with Thomas. He

was always trying to do hard things that most of the boys would not think of trying to do.

Most of the boys went to school to learn to read and write. Thomas could go to school but two or three months in his life, but he learned to read and write as well as any of the boys. This is because he taught himself, with the help of his good mother.

One time he read fifteen feet of books in the Public Library of Detroit, Michigan. He began at the bottom shelf and read every book. Then he read the books on the next shelf. When he had read fifteen feet of books someone stopped him. Perhaps he would have read every book in the Library if he had been allowed to go on.

Thomas Edison was a poor boy and had to earn money as soon as he was old enough to do so. When he was twelve years old he became a train boy on the Grand Trunk Railroad. His work was to sell books, papers, candy and fruit. Thomas did his work well but he did not care to spend all of his time in this way. Someone gave

Thomas some old type and a printing-press. He set up a work-shop in one corner of the baggage-car, and went to work to print a newspaper.

You will wonder what kind of a newspaper a little fellow like Thomas could print, so I will tell you. He found out all about what was happening on the Grand Trunk Railroad. Then he printed the news in his little paper. Thomas Edison's paper was no larger than the top of your school desk, but it contained interesting news and the passengers liked to buy it. Thomas charged but three cents for his paper, and printed one each week. It was the only paper that told about the news of a railroad, and Thomas soon found that the people were well pleased with it. He soon found that he was earning a good many pennies each week, also.

But one day a sad thing happened! Thomas set fire to the baggage-car!

The conductor was a quick-tempered man who did not spend much time in saying or doing kind things. He ran into the baggage-car and put out the fire. Then he had the engineer stop the train at the next station, and in less time than it takes to tell about it, Thomas found himself on the station platform. And about his ears came his type, his press, and all that he had had in his work-shop.

The train started up at once while Thomas stood alone on the platform. Thomas watched the train as it grew smaller and smaller in the distance and he was a sad young fellow. "I will have to start all over, now," he said, as he gathered up the things that lay scattered about on the platform.

Thomas Edison went home where his father let him set up a work-shop in the cellar.

Besides printing, Thomas Edison liked to study about e-lec-tric-i-ty. He had been in many depots and had often heard the ticking noise in the offices of the depot-agents. He knew that this ticking noise meant that someone was sending a message by e-lec-tric-i-ity, and Thomas wanted to learn all about it. He got a good book which he studied every day. The book was called Tel-e-gra-phy, which is a very hard name, but Thomas Edison did not care about this. He knew that the long word was only another way of saying that messages could be sent by electricity.

Thomas thought that it would be great fun to send messages to his friend who lived near by. One day he found a stove-pipe wire, a few old bottles and several other things that would be needed in order to send a message. "Now all I need is the electricity and I can send messages to my friend," he said.

Thomas was thinking about it when he saw old Tabby the cat coming along "Oh! I know where I can get the electricity!" cried Thomas. "I have often seen sparks coming from old Tabby's back. There will be enough electricity to send many messages."

Thomas caught Tabby and rubbed the poor old cat's back the wrong way to make sparks. I need not tell you what happened when Thomas did this because you know what your old cat would

do if you were to rub his fur the wrong way. I
need only tell you that Thomas could not get his
electricity from old Tabby the cat. Nor could
Thomas send messages to his friend along the
stove-pipe wire.

But Thomas Edison did not give up when
things would not go his way. "Some day when I
know more about electricity I will find out how
to send messages to my friend," he said.

In the meantime Thomas Edison worked
harder than ever and learned many things that a
young boy does not often know. He even found
out what it means to be a hero as you will see.

Thomas had just stepped on to the platform
in front of a depot one day when he saw a big
heavy freight-car coming along the railroad
track. On the same track not far from the moving car sat little Jimmie the station master's
two-year-old boy. Jimmie was playing with
some of the pebbles that lay about him. He
thought it great fun to throw the pebbles over his
shoulders.

44

Thomas saw the moving car and he saw little Jimmie. He threw away the bundle that he was carrying under his arm and dashed on to the railroad track. He seized Jimmie and carried him off the track a moment before the freight train reached the spot where Jimmie had been sitting at play.

If Thomas had been one second later he would have lost his life for the car touched the heel of his shoe just as he and Jimmie fell on to the next track.

Thomas was scratched but little Jimmie was not hurt at all. Oh how glad the station master was when he saw this!

Jimmie's father the station master knew a great deal about the hard study called Telegraphy that Thomas Edison liked so well. He told Thomas that he would teach him how to use a telegraph machine because of what he had done for his son Jimmie.

Then it was Thomas's turn to be happy! How

pleased he was! And how eagerly he listened to all that the station master told him!

It was not long before Thomas Edison knew what the station master knew and many other things as well. He kept on working with electricity, and by the time he was twenty-one years of age he had become known as an inventor.

Thomas Edison gave up telegraphy and spent all of his time working at inventions until there were hundreds of them. No doubt your father or mother or teacher can name many of these. Some of them have been very very useful.

Thomas Edison learned how to send messages to his friend and he learned many other things that were much harder.

If you have electricity in your houses you may think of Thomas Edison because it was he who worked many months in order that he might find a good way to use electricity in lighting houses.

When you listen to a phonograph you may think of Thomas Edison because he was its inventor also.

And when you are looking at moving pictures you may think of Thomas Edison for he was the inventor of the wonderful machine that makes the wonderful moving picture.

THE BOY WHO WAS HIS OWN TEACHER

IT was this way. There were sixteen children in the family. All of these children needed clothes. They needed food. Other things they would have to have. Mr. Franklin, their father, had very little money. So he took Benjamin out of school.

Benjamin was only ten years old but he was a bright boy. Mr. Franklin said, "Benjamin can teach himself. He is a smart little fellow. He can help me make candles, too."

Mr. Franklin was a candle-maker. He needed someone to twist the wicks and fill the candle-molds with melted tallow.

Benjamin staid home from school to help his father. Once in a while his father gave him pennies to spend. The pennies jingled in Benjamin's pocket, one morning, and Benjamin was very happy.

Down the street came another little fellow. He, too, was happy and well he might be. He had a bright tin whistle which Benjamin heard when he was afar off.

"What a fine whistle you have," Benjamin said to the little boy.

"Yes, I bought it at the store over there," said the boy.

Jingle, jingle went the pennies in Benjamin's pocket. Away went the owner of the pennies.

"Any whistles today?" asked Benjamin of the store-keeper.

"Yes, good ones," said the store-keeper. "How much do you want to pay?"

"I will give you all I have," said Benjamin, and jingle, jingle went the pennies again.

"Very well," answered the man. "Pick out any whistle you want."

It did not take Benjamin long to choose. His eye had been on the bright tin whistle from the very first.

"I will take this one," said Benjamin. Then

he gave the store-keeper the pennies that had been jingling in his pocket.

Benjamin took the whistle home. He showed it to his brothers. His brothers laughed. They knew how much the whistle was worth. "You should not have given the man all your pennies," they said. "You have paid too much for your whistle."

Benjamin Franklin often thought of this. He did not waste his time nor do things that would cost him dearly. "Don't pay too much for your whistle," he would say to himself.

Benjamin did not like the work in the candle-shop. He thought that he could make more money at something else.

Benjamin's brother was a printer. "You can help me for awhile. I will pay your board," the brother said.

Benjamin went into his brother's shop where he learned a great deal about printing. Sometimes he wrote articles and put them under his brother's door. His brother thought that they were good and printed them. Benjamin did not tell who wrote the articles.

After awhile Benjamin said to his brother. "If you will pay me what my board costs I will buy my own food."

The brother said, "I will do that if you wish."

Benjamin bought food. It did not take all the money that his brother gave him. With the rest Benjamin bought books. These he read at night after his day's work was done. He learned many useful things from them.

But it was not long before Benjamin wished to earn more money. He had heard of the large city of Philadelphia, and he made up his mind that he would go to it.

Benjamin reached Philadelphia early one morning. He was very hungry. A man came along and told him where to find a baker's shop.

Benjamin did not waste much time in getting to that baker's shop. He went as fast as he could and came out with three big rolls. One he ate as he went along. The other two he kept. There was one roll under each arm, and Benjamin looked very funny.

Benjamin did not think of that. I suppose he thought, "My, but this roll tastes good."

There was a very pretty girl standing in a doorway. Benjamin stopped eating long enough to look at her. He would have dropped all the rolls if he had known who she was to be. She was to be his own wife when they both grew up. They often laughed when they thought of the funny picture Benjamin had made with his three rolls.

Benjamin had not been in Philadelphia long before he became a good printer. After awhile he became the publisher of a newspaper. He published an almanac that people liked to read, too. He called it Poor Richard's Almanac.

Benjamin Franklin kept on studying all the time. He began to be looked upon as a very wise young fellow.

In those days people did not know much about e-lec-tric-i-ty. Now we light our houses with it.

We use it in many ways. Benjamin Franklin saw the lightning in the sky. He said, "I believe that the lightning can be made of use in the world. I will see if I can bring it down in a safe way."

Then Benjamin Franklin made a kite at the top of which he put a wire. This was to draw the lightning into the kite. The kite was fastened to a string at the end of which was a key. The end of the string held in Benjamin's hand was a silk ribbon.

When a storm came up Benjamin went out and flew his kite. The lightning flashed! Benjamin Franklin was not at all afraid. He hit the key a little and tiny sparks came from it. How glad he was! He knew then, that the lightning could be brought down from the sky.

Benjamin Franklin kept on making the lightning do new things. At last he learned how to carry it into a house on rods and wires. Then he made it ring bells and do many things.

The people thought this very wonderful. How

much Benjamin Franklin has done for us," they said.

The people were right. Benjamin Franklin taught himself useful things. Then he taught them to others.

A GIRL WHO HAD ANIMAL FRIENDS
THAT YOU AND I MAY SEE

S OME people think that poor children cannot
have any fun, but you and I know that this
is not true at all. No doubt, you could
name many poor children who are happy most of
the time. This is because there are so many fine
things in the world that do not have to be paid
for with money. Some children know how to
make use of these fine things.

That is the way it was with Rosa Bonheur the
little French girl.

Rosa Bonheur lived in a city called Bordeaux,
for awhile. Her father was an artist and the
people of Bordeaux did not have enough money
to buy many of his pictures. For this reason
Rosa's father was very poor and Rosa did not
have many of the toys that other girls had.

But Rosa did not care about this, for she had
many good times. She was happy when she

could play in the woods or meadows where she gathered beautiful flowers. And she always had some pet animal at home, which she loved as dearly as any child ever loved a toy. Sometimes it was a rabbit, other times it was a squirrel, or a stray kitten that had come to her back door. There was always some animal in Rosa's garden, and she could not feel poor with so many friends about her.

Rosa made good use of her animal pets, too. She liked to make pictures of her animal friends. When she was only four years old she would take her father's brush and make daubs with it. If you were to have seen these daubs of paint you would not have known what they were meant to be, but Rosa knew. "A squirrel," she would say, or "A rabbit." These were Rosa's favorite pets at that time, and Rosa liked to think that she had made pictures of them.

Rosa and her three brothers were very happy in Bordeaux, but the time came when Rosa's father had to move the whole family to Paris. This was because Paris was a larger city and Mr. Bonheur thought that he might be able to sell more pictures there.

The Bonheurs did not have a fine home in Paris. There was no garden and there were no fields about the house. Their home was up six flights of stairs and was not large nor even cozy. Some children would have been unhappy in such a poor home, and Rosa was a little unhappy at first, but this did not last long. Rosa had not been in Paris many weeks before someone gave her a beautiful sheep with long silky wool.

It may be that Rosa's father and mother did not want their little girl to keep the pet because there was so little room for it. But they gave their consent at last, for the woolly sheep spent two years with Rosa.

It must have seemed strange to the woolly sheep to have to lie on the floor of a house. Perhaps he would not have liked it very well if Rosa had made him lie there all the time. Rosa knew that the sheep liked to be near the ground where he could smell the sweet grass and nibble a bit now and then. Rosa could not carry him down the six flights of stairs herself, so she got her kindest brother to do so. There was a little grass in the back yard which the sheep nibbled with great pleasure until night came. Then Rosa's kindest brother always carried him back into the house again.

After awhile Rosa had other pets also. She had a pair of quails that walked about her bedroom, and she had some canary birds that had as pretty yellow feathers as you have ever seen.

Rosa did not like to see her beautiful birds shut up in a cage all the time so she got her kindest brother to help her out again. This time he made a net which he fastened to the outer side of the window so that the birds could be safely let out of their cages.

Rosa loved her animal friends so dearly that she made up her mind to buy a farm when she grew up. On this farm she said she would have one of every kind of animal in the world.

Her father laughed at these plans, but Rosa did not laugh. She was only sorry that she could not buy the farm and the animals that very day.

Before Rosa was twelve years old, her mother died, and the three youngest children were sent to live with some cousins. Rosa was sent to a boarding-school.

Here Rosa did not do very well. She was growing to be so fond of drawing her pets that she could think of nothing else. Like Michael Angelo, she drew pictures on her books instead of studying them. Her Arithmetic papers were never 100, and her Spelling papers were very poor. But her Drawing lessons were very good indeed, and when there were prizes for good drawings they always went to Rosa.

In a short time Rosa's father took her out of school and sent her to a seamstress to learn how to sew. Rosa's father would never have done this if he had known how unhappy it was going to make his little girl.

Rosa did not like to sew at all, and she could

not draw because she had a needle in her hand instead of a pencil. She kept thinking of her pets at home and wishing that she were there to draw their pictures.

Poor little Rosa! She pricked her fingers at almost every stitch and she became pale and sad.

At last Rosa's father came to visit his little girl, and Rosa threw her arms about his neck and begged him to take her home with him.

Rosa's father saw that she was beginning to look pale. He took Rosa home again and left her in his studio while he went about the city giving drawing lessons.

Oh how happy Rosa was now! She would take her father's brush and try to paint the things that he had painted. Sometimes she drew with a pencil or a piece of charcoal, or modelled the figure of an animal out of clay. From morning until night she drew and modelled.

Mr. Bonheur began at once to teach Rosa, and each day he became more and more amazed at her beautiful work.

If Rosa had been like her father she would have painted many different kinds of objects, but Rosa did not do this. Rosa liked to paint and draw animals best of all and spent most of her time with them.

One time she drew her pet goat and her father was so pleased with it he hardly knew what to say. Mr. Bonheur thought that this was the best drawing that his daughter had made, and told her about it.

Rosa was so glad to know that the picture of the pet she loved so well had pleased her father. She set to work at once to draw other pets until she had many good pictures.

One time Rosa Bonheur drew a picture of two rabbits eating carrots, and this was so good that some people asked her to let them hang it in the gallery where fine pictures were often hung.

Many people stopped to look at the picture of the rabbits while it hung in the gallery. If it had hung near enough to the floor the children would have surely tried to stroke the white coats of the

61

pet rabbits for they looked so soft and furry. Many people were pleased to see so good a picture.

But Rosa Bonheur wanted to paint still better pictures so she kept on working harder and harder.

Rosa was too poor to pay for models. After she had painted all of her own pets she had to walk many miles into the country each day until she found an animal that she thought people would like to see in a picture.

There were some oxen plowing a field on the side of a hill, one Spring morning. Rosa thought that they would make a very pretty picture, so she drew them.

You should have seen how real they looked in the picture! Some of the oxen were pulling harder than others. The ones that were nearest the plow were doing the most work, while the ones that were the farthest away, were not doing much at all.

Rosa noticed this at once, and did not forget to tell about it in her picture.

Another time Rosa found an ass that had pulled a heavy load and had then been turned out into a field to rest awhile, and to eat some fresh grass.

Rosa painted the picture of this ass, and she made him look just as tired as he looked while standing in the grassy field. He looked stubborn, too. You would have a hard time getting him to work any more until he had rested.

One day, when Rosa Bonheur had grown to be a young woman, she made up her mind that she would try to paint a good horse picture. She set to work to study horses, and for eighteen months Rosa Bonheur visited horse fairs and horse markets. She studied her own horses, too, as well as those of her friends.

When she had finished studying, she could draw horses that surprised even the people who owned them and she knew a great deal about them. She could draw a horse that would prance about in such a way that you would almost want to step out of its path, for fear of being trodden upon. And when she drew a horse that was standing still, you would think that someone had just said "Whoa" to it.

When Rosa Bonheur had studied horses until she could draw them as well as this, she made a picture of a group of them. She called the picture THE HORSE FAIR and she made it two-thirds as large as real horses should be. It was so large that she had to stand on a step-ladder while painting some parts of it.

Oh how hard Rosa worked on this picture, and what a wonderful picture it was! It was the best work that Rosa Bonheur had ever done, and people came from all over the country, to see it. Some men thought it so good that they offered to pay thousands of dollars for it!

This made Rosa Bonheur very happy indeed. But she was even more pleased to know that she could make pictures that looked just like the animals she loved so dearly.

A GIRL WHOSE TWO HANDS DID
WONDERFUL THINGS FOR HER

WHAT would you say if someone were to ask you to tell the most wonderful thing that you could do with one or both of your two hands?

Perhaps you would tell about being able to build a toy airship or run an automobile. Perhaps you would say that you could play well on the violin or piano. It might be hard to name the most wonderful thing that your two busy hands could do with their ten busy fingers.

When Helen Keller was a little girl it would have been very hard for her to have answered the question. This is because Helen Keller was blind, deaf, and dumb, and her hands were very wonderful indeed. They did the work of both eyes and ears, and it would have been hard to tell which work was the greater. Just how the little girl used her hands for eyes and ears you will know before you have finished this story.

Helen Keller was not always deaf and dumb and blind. When she was a tiny baby she could see and hear just as well as any child of her age. She could talk, too, in baby fashion. At the age of six months she said, "How d'ye?" and "Tea, tea, tea." A little later she learned to say the hard word, "Water."

I suppose she laughed when her mother played "Peek-a-boo," or when her father let her play "Ride-a-cock-horse." When she was tired her mother rocked her to sleep with soft lullabies that all babies like to hear on their way to Sleepy Town.

When Helen was one year old she took her first steps. Her mother had just taken her out of the bath-tub, and Helen was looking about with her bright little eyes. Suddenly she saw the shadows of some leaves dancing in the sunlight on the bath-room floor. Helen forgot that she was a baby just one year old. She left her mother's

arms and almost ran to the place where the
shadows were dancing. Then she must have become frightened, for she fell, and her mother
picked her up at once. After that, Helen learned
to walk quickly, for she had taken the first steps
which are the hardest, as you know.

Little Helen might have gone on learning new
things each day had not a sad thing happened.
She became very ill when she was nineteen
months old. For a long time everyone thought
that she would not get well at all. At last she
grew better, but the sickness had left the dear
little baby blind and deaf, as well as dumb.

You will not want to hear about the many sad
days that followed. Little Helen went about
most of the day clinging to her mother's skirts
and making signs to tell what she wanted.

Helen's father and mother were very kind and
did what they could to make their daughter
happy, but it seemed of no use. Helen wanted to
talk, and to hear others talk to her. She wanted
to know what was going on in the world, too.

Helen grew sadder every day until her only happiness seemed to be her father's beautiful garden. Helen lived in a little town in Alabama. Her house was covered with beautiful climbing vines and there were roses, honeysuckles, and many other sweet smelling flowers about the garden.

Helen could smell sweet odors as well as any child. She could feel things with her ten little fingers also. She was always glad to go into the garden when the flowers were in blossom. She would smell of them and touch their dainty petals. But for a long time she did not know the names of the flowers nor could she tell any of her friends about them. How she wished that she might talk to her friends in some way, or know what they wished to say to her!

One day Helen's father heard of a deaf and blind girl who had learned to read, and to talk with others by the use of her two hands. Helen's father made up his mind to get a teacher for his little girl, if it could be done.

In order to do this, he had to visit a distant city, and a few months later, a kind teacher went to live at Helen's house.

Then Helen Keller's happy days began. The kind teacher knew that her pupil's hands could be taught to do great things, and she did not waste any time in beginning the work of training them.

Very soon after she had come, the teacher gave Helen a beautiful doll. In the palm of Helen's hand she wrote the letters "d-o-l-l." She did this until Helen had learned to know the word.

After awhile Helen was taught to write the word "doll" in her teacher's hand. How happy she was then! She ran to her mother and wrote the word again and again. It was a new way of talking with people, and this is what Helen had always wanted to do.

In a short time Helen knew the words "pin," "hat," "cup," "sit," "stand," and "walk." Before long she learned that every object has a name. When she gathered daisies or buttercups she was taught to spell the words that stand for these beautiful flowers. If a little girl visited her, she at once learned the word "girl." If someone gave her an apple, Helen was taught to spell the word that stands for this good-tasting fruit. You see the kind teacher was helping Helen train her hands to take the place of eyes and ears, and the little girl found the task more pleasant every day.

After Helen Keller had learned to spell words, she was given slips of card-board on which were printed words in raised letters. These words made sentences which the little girl soon learned to read.

When she could read what was printed on the slips she was given a printed book with raised letters. Can you imagine how delighted she must have been with her first book? Most children are well pleased when they have finished reading from the blackboard at school, and are given a primer. Helen was even more pleased than this, as you may suppose.

Reading was not all that Helen could do. When she was ten years of age she began to learn how to talk. She would place her fingers lightly upon the throat or lips of the person who was speaking. This she did in order that she might find out what movement there was. Then she would try to make the same movement with her throat or lips. This was no easy task, but Helen would not give up until she had learned to speak. She could not talk just like other children because she could not hear whether or not she was using the right tone. But she was very glad to be able to say anything at all. She liked to talk so well that when there were no people about, she would talk to her toys, to the stones that lay upon the ground, or to the beautiful trees that grew about her pleasant home.

Helen Keller grew happier each day, for she was learning to do many useful things. The time came when she could even read books like "Little Lord Fauntleroy," "Robinson Crusoe," "Little Women," or "The Arabian Nights."

When she had been studying a number of years, she made up her mind that she would go to college. And you may be surprised to hear that Heller Keller did this very thing. She went to college and worked at hard studies like Physical Geography, French, German, and Greek History. When she was not studying she would draw, embroider, row a boat, ride a tandem bicycle, or play chess.

After a time Helen Keller was through college. Then she wrote interesting books that many people have been glad to read.

All this could be done by a blind and deaf girl because her two hands did such great things to help her.

A GIRL WHO LIKED TO HAVE FUN

IT was a beautiful day and Louise Alcott did not want to stay at home. Away she ran, down the road, far from her father's house. Soon she saw some children playing in a yard. Louise always liked strange children. "Hello," she said. "Hello," the children said. "Come in and play."

Louise liked to have fun. She went to play with her new friends.

The children had a good time all afternoon. After awhile it began to grow dark. The friends went into their house. They did not ask Louise to go with them. She was left all alone.

The lamp-lighter came along and lighted the street lamps. Louise wanted to go home but she did not know the way. She walked up and down the street. "Oh dear! Oh dear!" she cried. "I wish that I could go home."

Soon she saw a dog on a door-step. She sat down next to him. It seemed so good to have found a friend. Before long the dog went to sleep. Louise went to sleep, too. Louise rested her head on the dog's back.

By and bye the little girl was awakened by a loud bell. A man called out, "LOST————A LITTLE GIRL SIX YEARS OLD. WEARS A PINK DRESS AND NEW GREEN SHOES."

"Why, that means me," said Louise, getting up at once.

The man heard the voice. He was the town crier. Louise's father had sent him to look for the little girl.

How happy Louise was! How happy the town crier was to have found her! How very happy the father and mother were when they saw her!

Louise's father had a library. Louise liked books. She would go into the library and take down the biggest books. Then she would build houses and bridges. Sometimes she built walls and towers.

One time Louise's baby sister was playing on the floor. Louise built a wall around her. Then someone must have called, "Come out and play, Louise," for off she went. She left the baby sister inside of the high wall.

Little Lizzie was asleep when her mother found her. She was a new kind of prisoner.

Sometimes Louise and her friends played fairy stories. Once they played Jack and the Beanstalk. They had a squash-vine for the beanstalk. One of the boys was the Giant. Someone cut the stalk and down fell the Giant. He had a good bump, that time.

Sometimes Louise and her friends played Pilgrim. They took sticks for staffs and walked over the hill.

Louise liked to play with dolls, too. She could make pretty clothes for them. When she was twelve years old she hung a sign in her window. It read:

> DOLL DRESSMAKER
> LOUISE M. ALCOTT.

In the window Louise also put some pretty dresses and hats that she had made. The children liked the hats the best. Some of them would ask Louise to make hats for their dolls. Louise was very glad to do this. She would say, "What kind of a hat shall I make?"

Most of the children would say, "The ones in the window are the best kind. The feathers are so pretty."

"Very well," Louise would answer. Then away she would go for the feathers. Her father's chickens could have told us more about that.

Louise earned a good many pennies making hats. She thought it great fun to earn the pennies. She would say, "Some day I shall make a great deal of money."

Louise thought it fun to tell stories, too. She would tell them to her sisters after they were all in bed. Sometimes they would get frightened. Then they would hide under the covers. Louise would hide too. She would forget that the stories were not true.

When Louise Alcott grew up she wrote many long stories. She earned the money she had said that she would earn. One story was called "LITTLE WOMEN." The little women were her sisters and herself. You will like to read other stories that she wrote too. Here are some of them:

> LITTLE MEN
> ROSE IN BLOOM
> AN OLD FASHIONED GIRL
> JACK AND JILL
> UNDER THE LILACS.
> MY GIRLS
> EIGHT COUSINS
> MY BOYS
> LULU'S LIBRARY

A GIRL WHO LIKED TO READ STORIES
AND WRITE THEM

IT was story night at the school. The best pupils had been asked to write stories. These the teacher read to all the people.

Each time the teacher read a story, the people clapped their hands. For some stories they clapped louder than for others. When one story was read the clapping was the loudest of all.

People began to talk. "What a fine story!" they said. "Can a pupil have written it?" Everyone wanted to know who had done such good work.

At last Mr. Beecher called out, "Please tell us who wrote that story. It is such a good one."

"Your daughter Harriet wrote it," answered the teacher.

When Mr. Beecher heard this he was very much surprised. How pleased he was! And how glad Harriet was to see her father so well pleased!

Harriet made her father happy in many ways. Before she was six years old she had learned twenty-seven hymns. Besides this, she could repeat two long chapters of the Bible.

Mr. Beecher was a minister and liked to have his daughter learn verses from the Bible. He liked to have her write stories also.

Harriet did not read and write stories all the time. She liked to play too. You should have seen her doll. It was made of wood and had glass eyes that stared at you in a funny way. The paint was washed off its cheeks and its hair was badly out of curl.

Harriet thought that it was a very fine doll for it was one of her best friends. When she went to the woods the doll went also. When she wrote stories the doll sat beside her and kept very very still. When she gathered nuts or berries the doll was the first one to taste of the good things. At night the doll was tucked up in bed with its little mother.

Near Harriet's home there were fields, ponds and even woods, so that Harriet had many a good time out-of-doors. She liked to gather the wild flowers that grew in the fields. She liked to help her brothers sail their boats on the ponds. In the Fall she gathered chestnuts and walnuts in the beautiful woods.

On Sunday Harriet and her brothers went to church where their father, Mr. Beecher preached. They all rode in a big wagon with a skin thrown over the seat. The skin took the place of a cushion.

The two dogs went to church too. They tried to be quiet as all church-going dogs should be. One of the dogs did very well. Now and then he would snap a few flies but this did not happen often. He would curl up on the rug near the door and take a long nap.

The other dog did not do so well. Sometimes he walked down the aisle and looked at all the people. Then he would yawn out loud so that it was hard for Harriet to keep from laughing. The sermons in those days were long and the dog got tired. Once in awhile he would fall asleep and have a bad dream. When all was quiet, "Bow-wow, bow-wow," would come from the back of the church. Everyone would look around. One little girl always giggled. At last Harriet had to leave the dogs at home. You see, barking dogs do not make good church-goers.

On Sunday afternoons Harriet read Bible stories. She liked these very well but she also liked the books that she read on week days. THE ARABIAN NIGHTS was her best friend. She had found it in the attic while looking over some barrels of old papers. This fine story book was at the bottom of one of the barrels.

Harriet's father, as we have told you, was a minister, and wrote many sermons. In the attic he had several barrels of old sermons and pamphlets. Harriet liked to upset these barrels. Then the old sermons and pamphlets would fall out and Harriet could read the titles. Some of these were very queer and Harriet did not always understand them. Now and then she found something that she could understand, and this brought her great joy. When she found THE ARABIAN NIGHTS, one rainy day, you may know she was very very happy.

There were times when Harriet's brothers did not care to take Harriet with them when they went on their fishing trips or when they played games that boys liked to play. Then Harriet always got out her dear friend THE ARABIAN NIGHTS. She never got lonesome when she had this good story-book to read.

If you have ever curled up in a big chair with a good story-book, you will know why Harriet did not get lonesome when her brothers left her at home.

Sometimes Harriet took her friend THE ARABIAN NIGHTS upstairs into her father's study room. Here it was very quiet because Harriet's father went to the study room to write his sermons. Harriet's father always sat in his study chair and rested his elbows on a big table.

Harriet liked to sit in the big arm-chair that stood in one corner of the room. She kept very very still as she sat there. Sometimes she looked around at the rows of books that stood on shelves all about the walls of the room, from floor to ceiling. She tried to read the titles of the books that were nearest her. Most of the time Harriet had her friend THE ARABIAN NIGHTS with her. Then she read with great delight while her father wrote busily on a sermon.

One happy day Harriet's father brought home a new book of stories about Harriet's own country THE UNITED STATES, and Harriet loved her country more and more as she read about it.

Harriet's uncle was a sea-captain. When he came to visit, he often brought new books with him. These he read aloud to Harriet and the rest of the family. Harriet's Aunt Mary read some of the books aloud, also.

Harriet grew fast just as most boys and girls

do. When she had grown to be a young woman she married a man whose name was Mr. Stowe. She called herself Harriet Beecher Stowe.

After this, Harriet Beecher Stowe was very busy indeed, for it was not long before she had little children of her own. But she always found time to read good stories and even write them.

One day Harriet Beecher Stowe began to write a story. She wrote busily for many days until it was finished. It was such a long story it made a book, and Harriet Beecher Stowe called the book UNCLE TOM'S CABIN. It was about a negro named Uncle Tom, and was the best story that Harriet Beecher Stowe had ever written. All over the world people wanted to buy the book. People felt more friendly toward the negroes after they had read it.

Before many years had passed all the slaves were set free.

The story of UNCLE TOM'S CABIN had helped to free them.

A LITTLE BOY WITH A LONG NAME

A NOTICE was once posted up in the big city of London. The notice was printed in big letters. It said that a little boy was coming to play the clavier for the people of London. The clavier was the kind of piano that was used then.

The boy was eight years old. His name was Wolfgang Mozart. At least, this was a part of his name.

Wolfgang lived at a time when few children could play on the clavier. He had come many miles to play for the people of this big city. He wanted to earn money for his father who was very poor.

The people said "What! Can such a little boy make good music? It can't be true! We will go and see."

Then they went to hear little Wolfgang Mozart play. The hall was filled with people. Everyone looked to catch sight of the boy who was so young to play.

At last he came in. What a dear little fellow he was! He had such a beautiful face and his eyes shone with joy.

While he played, some cried, others smiled. It was the most beautiful music that many had ever heard.

A great many of the people gave the little boy beautiful presents. Wolfgang had so many things he could have started a shop. There were toys, candies, books and even laces and shawls.

A few of the people could not believe that such a little boy could play so well. They thought that there must be some trick about it. They invited Mr. Mozart and his son to visit them. They found some music that the child had never seen. This they asked him to play. He did so well they were ashamed. He even let them cover the keys of the clavier with a cloth. Then he played without being able to see any notes. After that, he made up pieces.

The people did not know what to think of it. The boys father was pleased. He said, "My little boy could play when he was but three years old."

Mr. Mozart spoke the truth. When the boy was only three, he could play little tunes. At four, he could learn a short piece in half an hour. When he didn't have any more music, he would make up some.

When Wolfgang Mozart was four years old, his father gave a party. Many friends came. One of these friends saw a piece of music on the clavier. The friend played the piece. Everyone listened. How very beautiful it was!

Mr. Mozart said, "I never heard that piece. Who wrote it?"

His friend said, "I found it on your clavier."

Mr. Mozart called his daughter. He said, "Did you write that piece of music?"

"No, father," she answered. "I did not write it."

Then Mr. Mozart thought of Wolfgang. "Surely my little boy did not write it," he said. "He could not write such a beautiful piece, for he is too young."

"Ask him," one of the friends said.

Mr. Mozart called the child. "What do you know about that piece of music over there?" he asked. As she spoke, he pointed to the clavier.

"I will show you," replied the boy.

Wolfgang sat down and played the music for Mr. Mozart and his friends. They all clapped their hands. Wolfgang was the one who had written the music!

In a few years the King asked Wolfgang to play for him. The little fellow pleased the King very much. The King's daughter was also pleased. The little boy would jump up into the lap of the princess and kiss her. He thought that she was a fine lady, for she was very good to him.

Wolfgang liked the princess very much indeed, but he liked his father the best of all. He would say, "Next to God comes papa."

Wolfgang Mozart went to play in London. We have told you about that. After awhile he left London. He went to other cities. Everyone was glad to hear him.

At one time Wolfgang was taken ill and had to stay in bed for a long time. "I will do as you wish," he said to the people who took care of him. "Will you do something for me? Get me a piece of paper, a pencil and a board. You can lay the board across the bed."

The little fellow's wishes were granted, and on the paper Wolfgang wrote beautiful music.

This was not the last time that Wolfgang wrote music. When he was well enough to be about again he kept on writing beautiful pieces. He wrote and wrote for many years. When he had grown to be a man someone counted his pieces. There were more than six hundred of them. Wolfgang Mozart had worked very hard, for he was only a young man when he died.

Now it is your turn to work hard, also. Wolf-gang had a long name and you will want to learn to read it. This is the long name: JOHANNES CHRYSOSTOMUS WOLFGANG THEOPHI-LUS SIGISMUNDUS MOZART.

A KIND NURSE

THEY named her Florence because she was born in Florence, Italy. Her last name was Nightingale.

Florence Nightingale lived in Italy, for awhile. Then her parents moved to England. They had a beautiful home. This time it was in the country.

Florence was a very happy little girl. She had many toys. Some people said that she could have as many dolls as she wanted.

Florence did not sew for her dolls nor did she go visiting with them. She liked to play that they were sick. Then she would care for them. Sometimes she tied up their legs or arms when they were broken.

There were many animals about Florence's home. When they were sick she cared for them, too.

In the woods near by, was a cottage. In the cottage lived a shepherd with a dog named Cap. The shepherd had no family. Cap the dog was all the family he had. Cap was a very fine dog. He never let anyone harm the sheep. He was fond of his master and tried hard to please him.

Florence was out riding with a friend, one day. They saw the shepherd in the field, but Cap was not there.

"Where's Cap?" they asked of the shepherd.

"Poor dog. I fear that I shall have to kill him," the shepherd said.

"Kill poor Cap!" cried Florence. "Why do you wish to do that?"

"Oh," answered the shepherd. "His leg is broken. Some bad boys hit him with a stone." The shepherd looked very sad. With Cap gone he would have no family at all.

"I am very sorry for you," said Florence. "At my home are many animals. When they are sick, I care for them. May I see your dog?"

The shepherd told Florence and her friend to

follow him. He led them up to the cottage where the dog was.

Florence got some water and bathed Cap's leg gently. She found that it was not broken after all. It was only badly bruised. Florence cared for the dog until it was well enough to tend the sheep again. The shepherd was glad that he would not have to lose his family.

Florence had many animal friends. Behind her house was a board walk on either side of which were tall trees. When Florence dropped nuts the squirrels would run down the trees and help themselves to a feast. Florence did not frighten the animals at all.

Peggy was a little gray pony. She, too, was one of Florence's friends. When Florence went into the pasture Peggy would run to meet her. She would put her nose into Florence's dress pocket and pick out an apple or a piece of bread. Florence did not often forget to put an apple into her pocket for Peggy.

When Florence was a little girl she liked to

care for her dolls and animals. But as she grew older she cared still more about being kind to sick people. She wanted to learn all about nursing so she read many books that told about it. After awhile she went to a nursing school where she learned useful things that a good nurse should know.

She went back to her father's home, and when she heard of sick people who were poor, she cared for them without pay. "I do not need any money," she said. Florence's father had plenty of money, and this was why Florence would not take any from the poor people.

Then Florence Nightingale visited hospitals in other countries. When she got back she tried to make the hospitals of England as good as the ones she had visited.

Finally a great war broke out, many miles from home. The winter was a cold one, and the soldiers were having hard times. Many were sick and without nurses. No one wanted to go.

At last Florence Nightingale made up her

mind. "I will go to nurse the soldiers," she said.

After many days she reached the far-away country. The soldiers were glad to see her. Florence was glad that she had come. Soon she had other nurses to help her.

Florence Nightingale helped to save many lives that cold winter. She was a kind nurse to the sick men. Many would have died if she had not taken care of them.

When Florence Nightingale went back to her home in England the people gave her a large sum of money because she had done so much for the soldiers. Florence Nightingale did not keep the money. She used it to pay for a training school where other girls might learn how to become good nurses also.

After awhile she wrote a book that told all about what to do for sick people.

A POOR BOY AND WHAT BECAME OF HIM

THERE once lived a very poor little boy
named Abraham Lincoln. He did not live
in a house like yours. His first home was a
log cabin.

The cabin had but one window which had no
glass in it at all. In winter the window was covered with wood. In summer it was left open.
Inside the cabin were three-legged stools, a table,
and a few dishes. In the winter the cold came
through the cracks of the cabin.

There were wild animals living in the woods
about Abraham Lincoln's home. Bears, wolves
and panthers ran about from place to place.
There were raccoons, and even fierce wildcats
and timid deer lived in the forest. Abraham was
glad that there were so many animals about.
His father hunted them, his mother broiled or
roasted them for supper, and Abraham helped to

eat them. In the winter when the cold winds swept through the forest, broiled or roasted meat tasted good to the Lincoln family.

Abraham's mother made corn cakes too. These were baked in the ashes and Abraham thought that they were very fine cakes.

It is no wonder that the fresh meat and cakes tasted good to Abraham, for he was such a hard worker. He was up with the birds in the summer, and up before the birds were awake, in the winter. All day long he worked as hard as he could. His father cut down the trees, his mother cut off the branches, and Abraham and his sister Sarah piled the brush into big heaps. Sometimes Abraham went hunting with his father, or fishing in the cool streams. He had to fetch the water for the family to drink, and help plant and care for the corn in the garden.

Abraham worked hard but he was out-of-doors most of the time, and the things that he did proved to be good for him. He grew tall and strong, and when he was seven years old, you would have thought that he was a boy of nine or even ten years.

When Abraham was eight years old his father moved the family to a new home in Indiana. This home was also in the midst of the woods and Abraham's father had to clear a place for his camp.

Mr. Lincoln built a half-faced camp. It was made of logs and was open on one side. On this side a log fire was kept burning night and day.

If you were to have lived in this house in the summer time you might have thought it very fine, but I am sure that you would not have liked it in the winter. Sometimes the wind blew so hard that the smoke from the fire blew right into the house, and the family had to go out-of-doors into the cold, to get away from the smoke. At other times the snow came in, and Abraham and his sister had to pull their deer-skin clothes tightly about them to keep warm and dry.

Abraham was busy here, just as he had been in his first home. He was learning to be a better hunter every day, and a better farmer, too. He was a great help to his father, and at the end of the first year Mr. Lincoln had time to build a new home that was better than the half-faced camp with its three sides.

Abraham's new home was not a cozy one for it had only the earth for a floor and a hole for a door, in which was hung an untanned deer's hide. The winds came through the cracks of this cabin, also, but it was better than the old one, and the Lincoln family was glad to have it.

Abraham's mother made good clothes for her husband and children, and these helped to keep them warm in spite of their cold house.

Abraham wore moccasins of deer-skin. His shirt was made of wool and cotton that his mother had woven and colored with a dye made of roots and bark. He had deer-skin breeches and a deer-skin hunting coat. On his head was a raccoon skin cap with a tail that hung down the back of his neck.

Abraham's clothes were warm but rough looking. They made Abraham look rather queer for he had "grown like a weed" and was tall and awkward.

But Abraham did not think about his rude clothes. He was growing to be a fine young fellow, always eager to learn new things.

There was no school to attend every day. Now and then a teacher passed through that part of the country and held school for a few weeks, and then Abraham and his sister were to be found among the pupils. One time they walked five miles to attend one of these schools.

Abraham and Sarah did not mind this. They would have been glad if the school had lasted longer than a few weeks, but it never did. When I tell you that Abraham went to school but four months in his life you will know that the teachers did not care to stay long in that rough wooded country.

Abraham would not give up trying to learn, just because there was no school. He wanted to learn to write well but he had no paper, for he was too poor to buy any. So he wrote on a shovel and for a pencil he used charcoal. When the shovel was covered he rubbed off the charcoal.

Abraham liked to read but he had only a few books, and there were no libraries. Abraham had to borrow books from people who had more than he. These he read at night by the light of the fire. When he was through, he put the books into his book-case. The cracks between the logs he used for a book-case.

After Abraham had put the books away he would go to sleep on his bed of dry leaves.

One night there was a heavy rain. It got into Abraham's book-case. One of the borrowed books got very wet.

"What shall I do? What shall I do?" cried the poor boy when he saw what had happened. "I cannot pay for the book for I have no money, but I am strong and I can work hard. I will work to pay for it."

Abraham went to the man who owned the book. "I am very sorry," he said. "The rain got into my book-case and almost ruined your book. I wish that I could pay for it but I cannot. I am too poor to do that. I will work for it. I will work as long as you wish."

The man said, "Very well, you may work three days."

Then Abraham worked for three days pulling corn. He was glad that the man would let him do something to pay for the book.

The Lincolns had not lived in their new home long before other settlers began to come. In a few years there was a store and a blacksmith shop. Once in a while Abraham had a chance to read a newspaper, too. This he enjoyed very much. He was getting the idea that there was much to learn outside of the small part of the country in which he lived.

For this reason Abraham was glad when a friend took him to New Orleans on a flat-boat. The boat was loaded with bacon, potatoes and other country produce which was exchanged for cotton, tobacco and sugar. Lincoln learned many things while on this trip and received eight dollars a month and his board.

A short time after this, Abraham's father moved to Illinois and Abraham worked at odd jobs on the farms about his home. The people liked to have Abraham work for them because he did his work well and was so very honest. He had strong muscles, too, and could work a long time without getting tired.

When Abraham was twenty-two years of age he was asked to go to New Orleans on a flat-boat again. Abraham was only too glad to make a second trip to New Orleans and he made good use of his time while on the way.

Abraham was beginning to feel that it would be better for him to go out and see more of the world, now that he was old enough to do so. When he returned to his father's home he told of his plans, and before many weeks had passed he had found a position in a country store.

Here he again won many friends by his honest habits.

One day a woman came into the store to buy some tea. Abraham made a mistake and gave the woman less tea than she had paid for.

He did not notice the mistake until the woman had left the store and gone to her home.

"Oh my!" he said when he found what he had done. "I have given the woman too little tea. She is poor and will need all the tea that she paid for. I will take it to her."

Abraham walked two miles into the country to give the woman the tea. It is not strange that the woman thought Abraham an honest lad.

Abraham had a chance to show that he was patriotic as well as honest. An Indian War called The Black Hawk War broke out, and Abraham Lincoln left at once to join the army. Some of the soldiers left at the end of the first term and returned to their homes. Abraham would not return until the war was over.

When he at last went back to the town in which he had kept the store, he found that everyone had heard about his good work in the war.

Abraham had been made a Captain and this was one reason why his work was so well known.

Abraham did not think much about what the people said. He was so very busy trying to decide what he should do to earn a living. The man who had owned the country store had failed, and Abraham had to find other work.

Abraham wanted to become a lawyer and a kind friend agreed to let him read his law books. Abraham was glad to do this. He studied so hard that he soon knew as much as many young fellows who had gone to school to study law.

At last Abraham Lincoln was elected a member of The Illinois State Legislature.

From this time on, he had better chances in the world, but he kept on working as hard as ever.

When he left the Legislature he went on with the law work in Springfield, Illinois, and after a few years he became a member of The House of Congress at Washington.

All of this time Abraham Lincoln had been

thinking a great deal about the negro slaves. While on his second trip to New Orleans he had seen people buying and selling slaves and he thought it very unjust and cruel. He made up his mind that he would always fight for their freedom.

When he became a member of Congress he did all that he could, but at that time he could not do much except make speeches about them.

Finally, Abraham Lincoln was made President of the United States and he then had a chance to do great things for the negro.

In less than five years every slave in the country was a free man!

And this was because there had once lived the poor boy named Abraham Lincoln.

A RICH BOY AND WHAT BECAME OF HIM

THERE once lived a rich little boy named George Washington. He did not live in a log cabin. He lived in a big house that was very cozy.

George's mother owned many things that were worth a great deal of money. One of these was a sorrel colt. It was a beautiful animal, but such a wild one! No one could ride it. When the colt grew up it would have little colts and they, too, would be worth a great deal. This is one reason why it had not been sold.

Mrs. Washington's son George was a brave boy and a good rider, as well. He wanted to learn to ride his mother's colt.

One day George was out in the pasture with the boys. "Boys," he said. "If you will help me get the bridle on to the colt, I will ride it."

"Oh George," the boys answered. "You will

be hurt. Do not try to ride such a wild animal."

"Please help me, boys," replied George. "I am not afraid. It is a shame that such a beautiful animal cannot be broken."

The boys helped to put on the bridle and George leaped up on to the colt's back.

Oh! Oh! How the colt jumped! How she plunged and reared! The rider held on more tightly but it was the end. Down fell colt, rider and all. The sudden leap had killed the beautiful colt that Mrs. Washington liked so well.

Mrs. Washington knew that George had been in the pasture. When he got into the house she said, "How are my fine colts this morning, George?"

Then George told what had happened. "Mother," he said. "I am very sorry. Your best colt is dead and I am to blame for it."

Mrs. Washington was angry at first, but she soon forgot her anger and did not punish George at all.

"I am sorry to lose such a fine animal. I wish

that it had not been my favorite horse," she said. "But I am very glad that you have told me everything. It pleases me to have a son who is truthful."

George was glad to know that his mother was pleased with him. He was glad when he found that his brother Lawerence was pleased, also.

George liked his big brother Lawerence very much. Lawerence Washington was a soldier and could tell good stories about brave men. George said that these were the best stories that he had ever heard. While his brother talked George wished. He had a soldier for a brother and a soldier for a grandfather. It is no wonder that George wished that he might be a soldier too. He thought that brave men were the best men in all the world.

There were years before George would be old enough to become a real soldier. So he got his friends together and they had a few play battles. The cornstalks that they used for guns did not shoot very well. It was hard to make a loud noise on the gourds that they used for drums. In spite of this, the soldiers fought bravely, and many battles were won.

George was a strong boy. He could throw a stone higher than some men. There was a bridge made of rocks near his home. This bridge was more than a hundred feet high. George threw a stone over this high bridge, one day. Then he climbed the rocks and wrote his name up on top.

George liked to have fun out-of-doors but he liked to go to school too. He went to a country school where he learned Reading, Writing and Arithmetic. George Washington did not have to write on a shovel with charcoal. He had pencils and a copy-book. George liked to write in this book, and he took great care to keep it as neat as he could.

After George had learned Reading, Writing and Arithmetic, he learned how to measure land. This is called surveying, and in George Washington's time a good surveyor could earn as much as ten dollars a day because there were not many who could do the work well.

George liked to survey land, even though there were times when he had to go out into the wilderness. Here his only food was the deer, wild turkey, or other animals that he could shoot. At night he wrapped himself in a blanket and lay down upon the ground to sleep.

At first George was not used to this because he had always slept in a cozy house. But he soon got used to the rough life and grew sturdier and stronger each day.

After a few years War broke out, and there was great need of brave strong men. Then George Washington the play soldier was ready to become a real one. He was even made a Captain, too. The wish that he had made when a little boy had come true.

At last a good President of the United States was needed, and George Washington was the first one chosen.

As you know, it is no easy thing to go to War.

Nor is it an easy thing to be a President. It took a brave man like George Washington to do the work well.

The people of the United States are glad that there was such a good man to be their first President.

They are glad that there once lived the rich little boy named George Washington.

A BRAVE BOY WHO DID NOT WANT TO BE
A SOLDIER

THERE was great happiness, one day, in the little cabin in Ohio where Mr. Jesse Grant lived with his young wife. A baby boy had come to live with them, a baby as chubby and healthy as you could expect one of his age to be. He was good, too, and only cried when he was hungry, tired or thirsty.

Mr. and Mrs. Jesse Grant thought their baby a fine little fellow. The good mother fed him with great care, and watched over him as only a mother knows how to do. The good father went about his work more busily than ever because he was so glad to think that there was one more in the family.

The child had been in the world but a short time when the father and mother began to think about giving him a name. Then there was trouble, for the mother wanted one name, and the father wanted another. The names that the mother liked did not suit the father, and the names that the father thought most fitting did not please the mother. Things went on in this way for some time, and the little child had no name at all except just "Baby."

At last the parents took the little boy to visit his two aunts and his grandfather and grandmother, who were surprised to hear that the baby had been given no name.

"Let us each write a name on a slip of paper and put the slips into a hat," someone said. "The name that is drawn from the hat first, will be the child's first one. We can choose his middle name in the same way."

The rest thought this a good plan, and the names were quickly written and put into the hat. Then the baby's mother drew one of the slips of paper from the hat. She opened the paper which had been folded, and read aloud the name "HIRAM," which was the name the grandfather had chosen. The baby's mother drew another

114

slip from the hat and found that it had the name "ULYSSES" written upon it.

The grandmother was much delighted when she heard this, because it was the name that she herself had chosen. "That was the name I wanted my little grandchild to have," she said. "It was the name of the great Greek warrior who was brave but also gentle. I do hope that our little Ulysses will be as gentle and as brave as his great namesake."

Hiram Ulysses only went on sleeping when his grandmother said this. At that time he thought more about sleeping and drinking milk than about deeds of bravery.

But the baby grew and grew. It was not long before he showed signs of becoming the brave boy his good grandmother had hoped that he would be. And for some reason people forgot that the first name was HIRAM and called the boy ULYSSES, or sometimes 'LYS for short.

Ulysses' father moved to a little village in Ohio, where he made skins into leather and also owned a good deal of land that had to be tilled. There were always horses about the place and little Ulysses played with them when he was scarcely old enough to walk. Sometimes he would hang on to their tails or manes. At other times he would try to get on to their backs. He was so short he had to stand on a box, and even then he was not high enough to climb easily. You would think that such a little fellow would be afraid of the big horses, but Ulysses was not at all afraid.

When Ulysses was six years old his father let him ride on the back of one of the horses whenever it was led to the trough to get water. In this way Ulysses learned to ride well, and was not afraid to ride the biggest horse that his father owned. The horses seemed to feel that a brave rider had them in charge. They soon learned to love his gentleness and firmness, and did not often try to disobey.

By the time Ulysses was seven years old he had learned to harness a horse. He had to stand

on a half-bushel measure that had been turned
upside down, and little Ulysses was only too glad
that he could make himself taller in this way.

When Ulysses was eight years old he bought a
colt of his own, and from that time he was never
without a horse of some kind. He kept on learning so much about horses that his father let him
do as he pleased with them. Ulysses fed and
watered his horses each day, and was often allowed to buy or sell one if he wished to do so.

When Ulysses was eleven years of age he had
driven about most of the country as far as forty
miles away, and a little later he had driven as
far as seventy miles.

This does not seem to be a very brave act to
the boys who live in Ohio, today. The state is
now built up well, and there are many good
roads. But when Ulysses Grant lived in Ohio,
the country was wild, and the roads were as dark
as pitch, by night. Most of them were rough, and
ran through dense forests that were very lonely.
And one could never be sure there was not an In-

dian standing behind a tree, getting ready to shoot with his bow and arrow. It took a brave boy to ride alone any great distance in such a country.

Ulysses was not afraid to risk his life on these journeys. Sometimes he carried leather to a distant city for his father. At other times he carried passengers from one place to another. There were mishaps at times, but Ulysses was never afraid to try the journey again.

One time Ulysses and a neighbor visited a place called Flat Rock where they met a man who owned a beautiful horse. Ulysses liked the horse so much he asked the man if he would trade it for the one that Ulysses had, if the man were paid a little extra money. The man needed the money and the bargain was made.

The horse had never pulled a wagon, but he seemed to be a gentle animal. Ulysses wanted to take the horse home at once, so decided to hitch him to the wagon which the old horse had drawn.

Ulysses and the neighbor who had made the journey with him, got into the wagon. All went well until they were about half-way home. Then all of a sudden a fierce dog came running out of one of the farm-yards, and snapped at the new horse's heels. In an instant the animal was kicking, and running as fast as he could. Ulysses cried, "Whoa! Whoa!" and held on to the reins tightly, but the horse would not stop. On he ran, straight toward a cross-road that had a twenty-foot ditch on the farther side. Ulysses' neighbor screamed and screamed, but Ulysses did not lose his nerve at all. He only pulled on the reins with all his strength and at last stopped the unruly horse at the very edge of the deep deep ditch.

The ride had been a little too swift to suit the neighbor of Ulysses. As soon as the horse had stopped the neighbor climbed out of the wagon, saying that he would try to get a ride on a wagon that went more slowly.

Ulysses said, "Very well. I will go on alone."

Then he tied his big handkerchief over the horse's eyes to keep him from seeing things that might frighten him. When he had done this, Ulysses drove on again. By this time the unruly horse must have learned that he had a firm driver for he did not run away again. When the neighbor reached home he was surprised to hear that Ulysses was safe in his own home and that he had not received so much as a scratch.

Ulysses often surprised his friends with the many daring things that he could do with horses. When he was twelve years old he could ride a horse at full speed, standing upon its back and holding on to the bridle. Sometimes he stood on but one foot, and this was even more daring.

Some children will think that the father of Ulysses was very good to let his son do as he wished with the horses. Mr. Grant was a good father, but Ulysses was also a good son. He did all the outside work that had to be done for his father's tannery business. Ulysses did not like to work inside the tannery but he was willing to haul leather to market, take care of the horses and cows, plough the land so that corn and potatoes could be planted, bring in the crops when harvested, and haul all the wood that was used about the house and tannery. All of this Ulysses did for his father, besides attending school, where he never missed a quarter.

The father of Ulysses was a well-to-do man for that day, but it was hard for him to get good hired men because there were so few people living in that part of the country. Mr. Grant was glad that he had a son who was willing to help so much. The father was also glad when he saw his son having good times, because he knew that they had been earned.

In summer Ulysses liked to go swimming and diving. In winter he skated and coasted with the other boys. There were a few good hills near the Grants' home, and Ulysses was always a daring coaster.

Some boys are brave, but they are also quarrelsome, and like to fight because they think that they can win. Ulysses was not this way. He tried to get out of a fight whenever he could. It is said that as a boy he entered into but one fight. This was when his cousin John made an unkind remark about George Washington whom Ulysses Grant had always loved and honored.

The cousin lived in Canada and liked the Kings of England just as boys who live in the United States like their Presidents. This would have been very well had not the cousin John said to Ulysses, "Your George Washington was a traitor when he fought the good King George."

Ulysses could not bear to have his hero called a traitor. "Say that again and I'll thrash you," he cried.

"I DO say it again," the cousin answered.

"Then I DO THRASH YOU," replied Ulysses.

What followed, you can well imagine. But after the fight was over the cousin never tried to say unkind things about George Washington or about any other hero that Ulysses loved. This was the last time that Ulysses ever fought with any other boy, also.

Most brave boys like to play soldier and try to beat the enemy. This was what George Washington always liked to do. You remember how he would gather his friends together and fight make-believe battles with some of them, using cornstalks for guns, and gourds for drums.

Ulysses Grant did not play soldier and he did not care to be one when he grew up. He did not even care to hear stories about the brave deeds that soldiers had done. Many of his father's and also his mother's people had been soldiers, and the father and mother could have told many stories about them.

When Ulysses was seventeen years old his father told him that he had been chosen to go to West Point where boys were trained to become soldiers. This was a great surprise to Ulysses and he did not like it at all. He wanted to get a good education and then take up farming for his work as a man. He did not wish to learn to be a soldier.

Mr. Grant would not take "No" for an answer. "My son," he said, "West Point is a good school and you can study there, even though you may not become a soldier later. Do this to please me, will you not, my boy?"

Ulysses loved his father and had always done what he could to please him. Besides this, Ulysses knew that he could visit several new cities on his way to West Point, and he had always enjoyed travelling about from place to place. With these things in mind, Ulysses said that he would study at West Point. "I will study there for awhile," he thought. "Then I will come home again and take up farming or some other work."

Ulysses had never been a bright boy although he had been a brave one. Some people were surprised when they heard that he had been admitted to the military school at West Point. Ulysses himself was surprised at this, but he entered the school with his mind set upon becoming a credit to his town and to his family.

At West Point Ulysses studied hard subjects like History, French, and Math-e-mat-ics. He also learned how to march, to drill, and to do other things that all good soldiers must know. Ulysses did not like any of the studies except Math-e-mat-ics. This study he liked very well. As time went on he changed his mind about wanting to become a farmer. He thought that it would be much better to become a teacher of mathematics.

In marching and drilling Ulysses was a good pupil, but when it came to working with horses Ulysses was the best pupil in the whole school. Ulysses always chose the wildest horse and took great pleasure in taming it. One of these was a horse named "Old York" which most of the boys were afraid to ride. Ulysses learned to ride the horse, and taught it to jump five and a half feet.

Ulysses learned to like West Point better than he thought that he would like it, but he was glad when he was at last through and could go back to his father's home. Ulysses planned to stay here until he could begin his work of teaching mathematics, but things did not turn out as he had planned.

Ulysses had been home but a short time when war broke out in Mexico, and the United States needed brave men to help win a victory. Ulysses did not like a soldier's life even after studying to be one. But when he found that his country really needed him, Ulysses made up his mind to join the army that was going to Mexico.

And then do you know what happened? I will tell you. Ulysses Grant went to war to fight for his country. He fought so bravely that he was made a lieutenant.

After awhile the Mexican War was over, and in a few more years the Civil War broke out. Again Ulysses Grant joined the army, and fought so well that he was made a Colonel. And before the Civil War had gone on for a very long time, Ulysses Grant was made the General of the whole Northern army, with more than **70,000** men under him!

If you were to have watched Ulysses Grant in some of the battles that he fought you would never have thought that he had not always wanted to be a soldier. You would only have thought, "How brave he is!" And you would have been right, for Ulysses Grant was one of the best soldiers that the United States ever had. He led his men into many battles, and helped to win a great victory.

When bullets were flying about him thick and fast, Ulysses Grant was just as calm as he had been when he was a boy riding along lonely roads at night, or mounted on a wild horse that no other boy would ride.

A few years after the Civil War was over, the people of the United States needed a new president. Then they chose Ulysses Grant, who became as good a president as he had been a general.

I wonder what the grandmother would have

thought if she had been living at that time? Do
you think she would have been sorry that she had
named the baby boy ULYSSES?

A FIGHTING BOY

TO begin with, Theodore Roosevelt was not strong but he made up his mind that he would do what he could to make himself as healthy as other boys. This was his first fight.

His father gave him the use of the wide back porch of his New York home and Theodore started in to learn to climb a pole for exercise. Try this sometime. You will see that it is not easily done at first. Theodore had to try it many times before he could climb without slipping. In this out-of-door gymnasium we can imagine a punching bag too. Theodore must have felt as if he had been running a mile a minute when he first tried to punch the bag.

Theodore Roosevelt's father was a well-to-do man. Besides his home in the city he owned a summer home three miles from the town of Oyster Bay where he and his family spent their vacation months. Here Theodore learned to swim, ride and row. Here he first learned to love the wild flowers and birds and to be eager to know their secrets. If a pair of robins built their disorderly mud-lined nest near the house, Theodore was not content with merely looking at the nest. He would watch the father and mother birds feeding the babies many many times each day and then he would find a book that told all about the robins. This he would read with great interest. Perhaps you have heard how a father robin carries fourteen feet of worms to his babies each day. After reading things like this, Theodore would watch the robins with greater interest than before. No doubt he admired the robin parents for their kindness. Perhaps he decided that he would be that kind of a father some day. At any rate, that is the kind he turned out to be. When he grew up he had five children of his own just like some of the father robins, and there were many people who admired him for the good care he gave his children.

Strange to say, not only living things interested Theodore Roosevelt. He learned about even the stones and rocks which he found in the places he visited. One time his parents took him to Europe. When they were getting ready to return home they found that Theodore had so many stones in his trunk there was hardly any room for his clothes at all. His mother decided that after all Theodore would be better off with a trunk full of warm underwear, clean stockings and other necessary articles of clothing. She threw the stones out of the trunk, whereupon Theodore filled his pockets. With his bulging pockets he looked for all the world like a boy just coming from an apple orchard.

When Theodore had grown to be a tall boy his father sent him to a wild place in Maine called Island Falls. At this place there lived a born woodsman named Bill Sewall who knew the wilderness and promised to take good care of Theodore. The old guide must have done this work well for Theodore never forgot the good times he had tramping and camping with the old woodsman. When Theodore grew to be a little older, he too, moved to a wild country. This country was in the far West and it was here that Theodore Roosevelt became a ranchman and hunter.

By this time Theodore Roosevelt had won his fight for good health. His face was tanned with the sun and wind and his muscles were strong and firm. Theodore had become a cowboy and he looked a great deal like the cowboys whose pictures you have seen. He wore leathern overalls and had a revolver fastened to his belt. Around his neck was a brightly colored handkerchief and on his head he wore a broad-brimmed hat which was of much use when he rode over the sunny plains.

Out in the wilderness Theodore Roosevelt built a log house in which he spent the night but he did not use this much in the daytime. From early morning until night he was busy out-of-doors raising vegetables, shooting game or animals for meat, cutting firewood, and even digging coal from his ranch to burn in the winter. Besides all this, he kept hundreds of cows which he had marked with a maltese cross. Like other ranchmen, Theodore Roosevelt had no fences for his cows. The cattle roamed around wherever they pleased, eating grass. Sometimes they wandered for hundreds of miles and would not be captured for months. You can plainly see why each one would have to be marked in some way. Twice a year Theodore Roosevelt would round up all the maltese cross herds. Then he would mark all the new calves and would send some of the fattest calves to market. The wagons which carried food would move to a new part of the country each day. Theodore Roosevelt and the other cowboys who helped him would drive in all the cattle they could find. This often meant a ride of over fifty miles in the morning. In the round-up Theodore Roosevelt would often have to sleep out in the snow, wrapped in blankets and tarpaulins, but with no tent to shield him from the freezing cold. This shows how well Theodore Roosevelt had won his fight to become strong and healthy.

Perhaps it was because he had won this fight so well that Theodore Roosevelt was encouraged to fight for other things. The people of New York elected him Police Commissioner which meant Head Policeman. Theodore Roosevelt had a chance to fight for millions of people then. He wanted the city of New York to become a safer and better place, and he put up a good fight to bring this about.

People heard about the good work he had done in New York, and they made him the President of the United States. Then once more, Theodore Roosevelt had many people to work for, and battles to fight.

To be sure, Theodore Roosevelt was no longer a boy, as far as age goes. He had become a man. But folks who knew him best said that he always remained a boy at heart. Perhaps this was because he played with his own boys so much and was so full of fun. Theodore Roosevelt taught them to box, swim, row and ride. He gave them animals and pets of many kinds. Before the boys grew up they had had a live bear, a lion, a hyena, a wild cat, a coyote, two parrots, an eagle, a barn owl, several snakes, a lizard, a zebra, a kangaroo, flying squirrels, rabbits, guinea pigs, as well as dogs of many kinds.

With four lively boys and so many interesting pets it was no wonder that Theodore Roosevelt could not feel "grown up." He was still a boy— a fighting boy, as he had always been.